W9-CNO-387

We Love Spring!
BABY ANIMALS ARE BORN

By Delores Soltaire

Gareth Stevens
PUBLISHING

Please visit our website, www.garethstevens.com. For a free color catalog of all our high-quality books, call toll free 1-800-542-2595 or fax 1-877-542-2596.

Cataloging-in-Publication Data
Names: Soltaire, Delores.
Title: Baby animals are born / Delores Soltaire.
Description: New York : Gareth Stevens Publishing, 2017. | Series: We love spring! | Includes index.
Identifiers: ISBN 9781482454680 (pbk.) | ISBN 9781482454710 (library bound) | ISBN 9781482454703 (6 pack)
Subjects: LCSH: Animals–Infancy–Juvenile literature.
Classification: LCC QL763.S65 2017 | DDC591.3'9–dc23

First Edition

Published in 2017 by
Gareth Stevens Publishing
111 East 14th Street, Suite 349
New York, NY 10003

Copyright © 2017 Gareth Stevens Publishing

Editor: Ryan Nagelhout
Designer: Samantha DeMartin

Photo credits: Cover, p. 1 sevenke/Shutterstock.com; p. 7 Cynthia Kidwell/Shutterstock.com; pp. 5 (fawn), 9, 24 (fawn) Betty Shelton/Shutterstock.com; pp. 5 (gosling), 11, 24 (gosling) Richard Fincher/Shutterstock.com; pp. 5 (chicks), 13 PCHT/Shutterstock.com; pp. 5 (calves), 15, 24 (calves) Smileus/Shutterstock.com; pp. 5 (cubs), 17 Giedriius/Shutterstock.com; pp. 5 (bunnies), 19 BogdanBoev/Shutterstock.com; p. 21 Nina B/Shutterstock.com; pp. 5 (kids), 23 Rita Kochmarjova/Shutterstock.com.

Printed in the United States of America

CPSIA compliance information: Batch #CW17GS: For further information contact Gareth Stevens, New York, New York at 1-800-542-2595.

Contents

Spring Babies 4

All About Deer 6

For the Birds 10

Cows and Milk 14

Baby Bunnies 18

Words to Know 24

Index 24

Many animals have babies in spring!

5

Deer have babies
in spring.

Baby deer are called fawns.
They have white tails.

Baby geese are called goslings.

Baby chickens are chicks.
They are very soft.

Baby cows are called calves.
They love milk!

Baby bears are called cubs.

Baby rabbits are bunnies.

19

Some goats are
born in spring.

Baby goats are kids!

Words to Know

calves

fawn

goslings

Index

bunnies 18

cubs 16

chicks 12

deer 6, 8